W9-DIH-370

AMAZING REPTILES

# Chameleons

by Christy Devillier

**Content Consultant**
Edward L. Stanley, PhD
Department of Vertebrate Zoology and Anthropology
California Academy of Sciences

**Core Library**

An Imprint of Abdo Publishing
www.abdopublishing.com

www.abdopublishing.com

Published by Abdo Publishing, a division of ABDO, PO Box 398166, Minneapolis, Minnesota 55439. Copyright © 2015 by Abdo Consulting Group, Inc. International copyrights reserved in all countries. No part of this book may be reproduced in any form without written permission from the publisher. Core Library™ is a trademark and logo of Abdo Publishing.

Printed in the United States of America, North Mankato, Minnesota
042014
092014

Cover Photo: Peter Krejzl/Shutterstock Images
Interior Photos: Peter Krejzl/Shutterstock Images, 1; Shutterstock Images, 4, 24, 32, 45; Stefan Huwiler/Glow Images, 7; SuperStock/Glow Images, 9; Natali Glado/Shutterstock Images, 10, 43; Nomad/SuperStock, 12; Biosphoto/SuperStock, 14, 36, 38; Animals Animals/SuperStock, 16; Chantelle Bosch/Shutterstock Images, 18; Frans Lanting/Mint Images/ Glow Images, 21; Juniors Bildarchiv/Glow Images, 23; Ahmed Maher/ Shutterstock Images, 26; Red Line Editorial, 28; Strauss/Curtis/Corbis/Glow Images, 30; Anthony Bannister/Evolve/Photoshot/Newscom, 34

Editor: Mirella Miller
Series Designer: Becky Daum

**Library of Congress Control Number: 2014902275**

**Cataloging-in-Publication Data**
Devillier, Christy.
 Chameleons / Christy Devillier.
   p. cm. -- (Amazing reptiles)
Includes bibliographical references and index.
ISBN 978-1-62403-370-4
1. Chameleons--Juvenile literature.    I. Title.
597.95/6--dc23

                                        2014902275

# CONTENTS

# CHAPTER ONE

# A Most Unusual Lizard

I t is a warm day in the rain forest. A green chameleon sits with its feet and tail gripping a tree branch. Without moving from its spot, the chameleon shoots its sticky tongue out to snag a grasshopper. It rotates one eye forward and the other eye backward. The chameleon's eyes work independently from one another. They spot a meat-eating shrike. The chameleon stays still and becomes

Scientists continue to discover new species of chameleons and learn more about these amazing reptiles each year.

5

darker, helping it to hide from the fierce bird. The chameleon is well disguised as it sits among the tree leaves. The shrike eventually flies away. The chameleon survives another day, thanks to its ability to camouflage itself.

Chameleons are reptiles that have been living on the earth for more than 50 million years. Scientists have identified approximately 200 species of chameleons. And there are more species scientists have yet to discover.

The chameleon family is divided into two groups. The first group consists of large, colorful, long-tailed chameleons that live mostly in trees. Chameleons in the second group are small, dull-colored, short-tailed, and live on the ground.

## Shape and Size

Most chameleon species have a flattened body shaped like a leaf. This shape helps chameleons warm themselves in the sun. They can also easily disguise themselves among leaves.

Not all chameleons are bright and colorful. Some species, such as the stump-tailed chameleon, have dull coloring.

Most chameleons grow to be between two to ten inches (5 to 25 cm) long. The smallest chameleon is the *Brookesia micra* from Madagascar. It grows to be approximately one inch (3 cm) long. The largest chameleon is also from Madagascar. The Parson's chameleon grows to be approximately 27 inches (69 cm) long. Large species can weigh more than one pound (0.5 kg).

## Chameleon Teeth

Chameleons' teeth sit on the top edges of their jaws. Chameleons use their teeth to hold onto food. They also use their teeth to help them crush or chew their food. Some chameleons may tear their prey into smaller chunks. Chameleons only develop one set of teeth in their lifetime.

## Changing Colors

Scientists used to believe chameleons could change their coloring and patterns to match their background perfectly. Now scientists know this is not true. Some chameleons can become lighter or darker to hide from predators, however. Color change is also linked to communication. Each chameleon species has its own range of colors and patterns.

## More Unique Features

Chameleons are special in other ways. They can rotate their bulging eyes to look in two directions at once. Chameleons can also catch prey from a distance because their tongues can extend to be as long as their bodies.

A chameleon tightly grips a branch with its unusual toes.

With fused toes and a tail that can grab onto objects, chameleons are built to climb branches. They have five clawed toes on each hand. The five toes are divided into two groups. Three of the toes are joined together on one side of each foot. The other two toes are on the other side of each foot. Some chameleon species also have a long tail they use to grab and hold things. These chameleons can latch onto branches using their tail like a fifth foot.

# CHAPTER TWO

# Chameleon Life

Chameleons are solitary animals. They do not live in groups or families. They are very territorial. Chameleons protect the area they live in from other chameleons. They only spend time together to mate.

When two male chameleons meet, they try to scare each other away. Each one becomes brightly colored. They may also hiss and bite each other.

It is very rare to see more than one chameleon in the same area unless it is mating season.

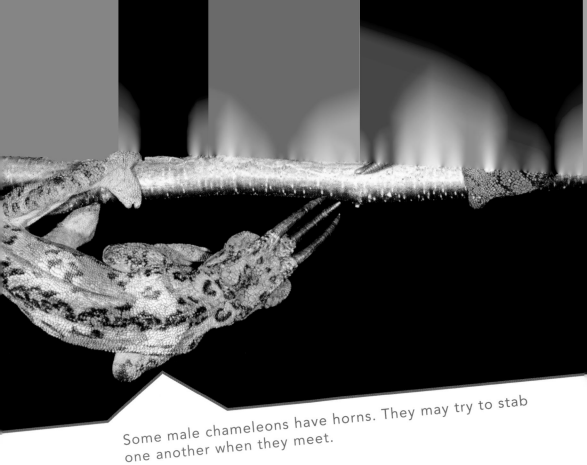

Some male chameleons have horns. They may try to stab one another when they meet.

Some chameleon species swell up to make their bodies bigger and puff out their throats. The chameleon that does not back down shows bright colors, while the loser shows dark colors.

## Mating

Chameleons also use color to communicate how they feel about mating. Some male species show bright colors when they want to mate. A female shows bright colors when she does not want to mate. This is a warning to stay away. She may also open her mouth widely and hiss until the male goes away. A female that is ready to mate will show darker colors.

Small species, like the montane jewel chameleon, are ready to mate at three months old. Larger species mate when they are older. Parson's chameleons mate at approximately 18 months.

## Nests and Eggs

Most chameleon species lay eggs. Females dig a shallow hole in the ground to make a nest where they can lay their eggs. A batch of eggs is called a clutch. The female chameleon leaves the nest after laying her eggs. Female Meller's chameleons lay one clutch each year. They may have up to eight clutches during their lives. The veiled chameleon can lay up to 16 clutches in its lifetime.

Chameleon egg clutches range from 2 to 60 eggs, but they can be larger. The size of the clutch depends on the size of the species. The small

A female chameleon covers its nest with soil, sand, leaves, or twigs.

*Brookesia micra* species may only lay two or three eggs. The medium-sized Fischer's chameleon may lay between 14 to 20 eggs at a time. Other medium-sized chameleons can lay as many as 30 eggs. Parson's chameleons lay up to 60 eggs.

The eggs of small chameleon species hatch in approximately 45 to 50 days. Eggs from larger chameleons can take 5 to 14 months to hatch.

# Baby Chameleons, Born Ready

Like many other reptiles, chameleons do not raise their babies. The mother lays her eggs in the nest and leaves it. Young chameleons know how to hunt and take care of themselves when they hatch. Most young chameleons have dull coloring. This helps them hide from predators. Young chameleons leave the nest and begin hunting for food immediately after hatching. They grow quickly.

## Life Span

Chameleon species have a range of life spans.

## Live Birth Instead of Eggs

Some chameleon species carry eggs inside their bodies and give birth to live young. This is true for Jackson's chameleon. The female gives birth about six to nine months after mating. She has between 7 and 30 babies at one time. Newborn chameleons are wrapped in a membrane, which they break open. Jackson's chameleons sometimes give birth two times after only mating once. The second birth happens a few months after the first.

Young chameleons may stay near the nesting area for a few days before moving away from their brothers and sisters.

The carpet chameleon lives between one and two years. Parson's, veiled, and Oustalet's chameleons live between five and eight years in the wild. Chameleons' life spans are longer in captivity. Veiled chameleons may live for ten years in captivity, while Parson's chameleons can survive for twenty years.

## A Short Life

The Labord's chameleon has a short life span. It stays inside its egg for eight to nine months. The eggs hatch in November. These chameleons only live for four or five months after hatching. Scientists believe their short life span is due to the extreme weather changes in southwestern Madagascar, where they live.

## FURTHER EVIDENCE

There is quite a bit of information about chameleon life cycles in Chapter Two. It covered mating and young chameleons. If you could pick out the main point of the chapter, what would it be? What evidence was given to support that point? Visit the website below to learn more about chameleons' life cycles. Choose a quote from the website that relates to this chapter. Does this quote support the author's main point? Does it make a new point? Write a few sentences explaining how the quote you found relates to this chapter.

### Say It with Color
www.mycorelibrary.com/chameleons

# Stealth Hunters

**A**lmost all chameleons hunt for food during the day. When they spot something to eat, such as berries, leaves, fruit, or insects, chameleons focus both of their eyes on it. This helps them judge how far away their food is. Chameleons may also rock back and forth. Scientists believe this helps chameleons mimic a branch in the wind. These movements break up their image to fool predators.

A chameleon's eyes move independently from one another. A chameleon can hunt for prey with one eye and watch its environment with the other eye.

After judging the distance of its prey, a chameleon shoots out its long tongue. This grabs the insect and brings it back to the chameleon's mouth. The capture happens in the blink of an eye. Chameleons propel their tongues forward at a speed of 13.4 miles (21.6 km) per hour.

A chameleon chews its meal before swallowing. With powerful jaws and teeth, a chameleon can easily crush insects with tough shells and other small animals.

## Meals Large and Small

Almost all chameleons eat insects. They eat grasshoppers, locusts, beetles, butterflies, moths, and mantises. A panther chameleon can eat as many as

A chameleon can sometimes stretch out its tongue longer than its body to catch prey.

20 grasshoppers in a day. Larger chameleons also eat birds, frogs, lizards, and small mammals.

Small, ground-dwelling chameleons hunt among leaves on the forest floor. They eat ants, mites, termites, and other tiny bugs. The veiled chameleon and the Namaqua chameleon eat plants when water is scarce. They do this to get water from the plants. Chameleons rarely drink from ponds or standing water. Instead they lap up dewdrops and rainwater collected on plant leaves.

## Whip Tongues

A chameleon's tongue is speedy. It has a round tip and many muscles. When still, the tongue is tightly folded like a spring inside the mouth. The muscles squeeze and shoot out quickly. The tongue pad has sticky saliva and a cup-shaped tip at the end that work together to trap prey.

Desert chameleons are able to eat creatures with venomous stingers. When capturing wasps or scorpions, they aim their tongue away from the stinger. They chew off and spit out the parts of the prey with venom. Then the chameleons eat the nonvenomous parts.

## Color Is Skin Deep

Chameleons' ability to change color helps them catch prey. Chameleons are known for changing colors quickly. They may change colors many times throughout the day for different reasons. Chameleons change colors depending on light, temperature, and mood. Chameleons may turn pale when they are resting. They have a darker, dull color when they

Chameleons are able to eat many kinds of insects.

are cold. Chameleons turn lighter after warming themselves in the sun.

Changing color also helps chameleons communicate with each other. Chameleons show bright colors when they are excited, angry, or scared. Most chameleons are green or brown when they are calm.

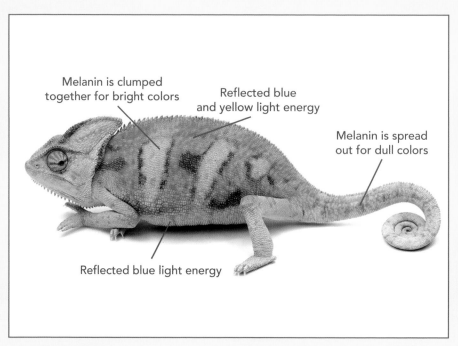

Melanin is clumped together for bright colors

Reflected blue and yellow light energy

Melanin is spread out for dull colors

Reflected blue light energy

## Color-Changing Skin

Chapter Three explores why and how chameleons change color. This diagram offers an up close look inside a chameleon's skin. How do pigment cells and other skin cells help chameleons change color? How do chameleons use color to communicate with each other?

A chameleon changes color using special cells in its skin. Below its transparent outer skin are two layers of pigment cells. The pigment cells in the top layer are red and yellow. The bottom layer has cells that reflect light, often turning the skin blue. When this blue light shines from the bottom layer through the red pigment cells, the chameleon's skin looks purple. If blue light shines through the yellow pigment, the skin looks green. Further down is another layer of melanin, which has black pigment. When the melanin clumps together, the chameleon's colors become bright. The color is less bright when the melanin spreads out.

## EXPLORE ONLINE

The focus in Chapter Three was on chameleons' hunting and eating habits. It also gives details on their unique tongues. The website below focuses on the same subjects. As you know, every source is different. How is the information from the website different from the information in this chapter? What information is the same? How do the two sources present information differently? What can you learn from this website?

### Cold-Proof Tongue
www.mycorelibrary.com/chameleons

# CHAPTER FOUR

# Madagascar and Beyond

T he island of Madagascar is home to approximately one-half of all chameleon species in the world. Madagascar is off the east coast of Africa in the Indian Ocean. Chameleons can also be found on other islands in the Indian Ocean. Many other chameleon species live in Africa. They also live in Saudi Arabia, Yemen, southern Europe, India, and Sri Lanka.

Many chameleon species live in the warm climate of Madagascar.

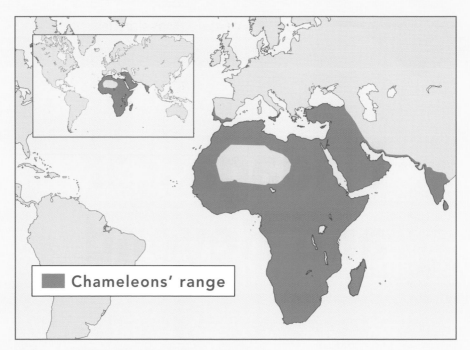

**Where Wild Chameleons Live**

This map shows the native homes of wild chameleons. Most species live in Madagascar and Africa. They can be found in other areas too. Why do you think chameleons live in these parts of the world? What do these areas have in common? Describe a few different chameleon habitats.

## From Rain Forests to Deserts

Chameleon habitats range from wet rain forests to dry deserts. Approximately two-thirds of all chameleon species live in tropical jungles and leafy forests. Chameleons can be found in drier, less wooded areas too. Some species live in Africa's grasslands and scrublands. They roam in bushes and tall trees.

Some chameleons have a large range and can live in many habitats. The flap-necked chameleon lives throughout southern and central Africa. It lives in forests and grasslands. When the weather is cold and dry, it hides in burrows or holes in trees.

Some chameleons only live in one tiny area. The habitat of a *Brookesia micra* chameleon is only one square mile.

Most chameleons are arboreal. This means they hunt, mate, and sleep

## No Ordinary Island

Madagascar is the world's fifth-largest island. It is almost the size of Texas. This piece of land was once part of the African continent. It broke away approximately 160 million years ago. As a result, Madagascar is home to wildlife that lives nowhere else on Earth. Lemurs, chameleons, the flying fox bat, the catlike fossa, the spear-nosed snake, the tomato frog, and the comet moth all live there.

The forest offers many places for a chameleon to hide from predators.

in trees and shrubs. The forest has many insects for chameleons to eat too.

Some chameleon species live on the forest floor. Most of these chameleons are brown, which helps them stay camouflaged among the leaves. They climb onto shrubs and plants to sleep at night.

The Namaqua chameleon lives in the Namib Desert in Africa. This chameleon is very different from its tree-dwelling cousins. The Namaqua lives on the ground. To prevent overheating, it digs in the

## Chameleons as Pets

Chameleons are good pets for owners who have experience taking care of them. These colorful reptiles are fun to watch, but they need special care. A good chameleon habitat must have the right amount of light, heat, and humidity. They need large cages filled with leaves and branches. Pet experts recommend buying chameleons raised in captivity, not from the wild. Many wild chameleons become sick and can die outside their natural habitat. Two species that do well as pets are the veiled chameleon and the panther chameleon.

With longer legs, a shorter tail, and toes that can spread out, the Namaqua chameleon can run fast and chase prey.

sand to find a cool spot. It can also lift its body off the hot sand by straightening its long legs. Changing to a lighter color also helps the Namaqua chameleon stay cool in the hot desert.

STRAIGHT TO THE SOURCE

Only 8 percent of Madagascar's original forests remain. Wildlife photographers Chris Mattison and Nick Garbutt explain why this is a problem for some chameleon species:

> Many species have extremely specific habitat requirements that restrict their natural range. Some like Parson's chameleon . . . and the lance-nosed chameleon . . . appear to prefer lowland rain forests, especially along streams, whereas species like Furcifer campani and C. hilleniusi are high-altitude specialists that are restricted to isolated montane outposts. Similarly . . . the Malagasy leaf chameleons are leaf-litter, forest-floor dwellers and inextricably tied to untouched native forests. None can survive in secondary forest. Any degradation to the habitats of these less-tolerant species would ultimately result in their extinction.

Source: Chris Mattison and Nick Garbutt. Chameleons. Buffalo, NY: Firefly Books, 2012. Print. 76.

## Back It Up

Review this passage closely. The authors of this passage are using evidence to support a point. Write a paragraph describing this point. Then write down two or three pieces of evidence the authors use to make their point.

# CHAPTER FIVE

# Danger and Defense

Chameleons face many kinds of enemies. Adult chameleons are prey for snakes, birds, mongooses, fossas, and other meat-eating animals. Honey badgers, monitor lizards, and bush pigs eat chameleon eggs. Chameleon hatchlings are prey for frogs, rats, insects, and spiders.

Boomslang snakes can spot camouflaged chameleons that are not moving and will attack them.

Vangas are large predatory birds with strong, hooked beaks.

## Snake Alert

Many arboreal snakes hunt chameleons. Cat snakes and the fandrefiala hunt chameleons in Madagascar. Cat snakes hunt for small and medium-sized chameleons at night. Fandrefialas kill large chameleons, including Parson's chameleons and Oustalet's chameleons.

## Feathered Enemies

Hornbills, lizard buzzards, and shrikes are African birds that prey upon chameleons. Chameleons in

Madagascar must look out for vangas. Their beaks can easily tear a chameleon apart.

## Defense

A chameleon's best defense against predators is hiding. Its color, body shape, and slow movements help it stay hidden. When an enemy is nearby, some species can become lighter or darker to blend in with their surroundings. They may also move to another side of a branch to hide from a predator.

### Fearsome Shrikes

Shrikes are also called butcherbirds. These birds have a unique way of killing their prey. They wedge chameleons and other animals in between tree branches and onto thorns. Shrikes and bush-shrikes can kill prey much larger than themselves. Bush-shrikes use their strong, hooked bills to overtake flap-necked chameleons. Shrikes may eat their prey right away or save it for later.

If hiding does not work, some large chameleon species try to scare predators away. Flap-necked, Oustalet's, and panther chameleons make

Some chameleons lie down on their backs and pretend to be dead when a predator is near.

their bodies flat. They open their mouths wide to show the bright color inside. These chameleons also hiss, bite, and raise their flaps to scare away enemies.

When danger is near, some chameleon species drop from their perches to escape predators. The only species that runs from enemies is the Namaqua chameleon.

## Keep Wild Chameleons Wild

Another danger to chameleons is the pet trade. Only a small number of chameleon species can survive outside of their natural habitats. Some people want to sell and buy rare species only found in the wild. From 1993 to 1998, more than 476,000 chameleons were taken from their habitats in Africa for the pet trade. It is likely that very few of these chameleons survived. It is now illegal in some countries to remove certain chameleon species from the wild.

## Losing Ground

Habitat loss is the main threat chameleons face across the world. Forests once covered most of Madagascar. Most of these wooded areas are now gone because humans cleared them for fields and towns. When people cut down forests, chameleons lose their homes. Some chameleon species can only survive in native forests. These species will die out when their habitats are gone. These chameleons are endangered and are at risk of becoming extinct. Some endangered species are the Belalanda chameleon, Smith's dwarf chameleon, and the tiger chameleon.

## New Species Found

Four new dwarf chameleon species were found in 2012 in Madagascar. They are among the smallest reptiles in the world. These chameleons are brown. They show a white stripe across their back when they are under stress. Dr. Frank Glaw is the reptile specialist who discovered them. He says habitat loss is a danger to these tiny chameleons.

## Saving the Chameleon

Chameleons are an important part of their habitats. They keep insect populations in check. Chameleons are also a good food source for snakes. The loss of chameleons would impact many other animals. Not all chameleons are endangered. But it is important to take care of all chameleons and their habitats.

Chameleons have been around for millions of years. Humans must learn more about chameleons and work to protect their habitats. These efforts will help chameleons survive in the wild for many years to come.

Scientists noticed one dwarf chameleon species reacted differently to two different predators. Scientists discuss the chameleons' efforts to hide:

*Chameleons consistently showed better background colour matching in response to birds than snakes, but even so, appear significantly more camouflaged to the snake visual system because snakes have poorer colour discrimination. There are two potential explanations for this pattern. The first is that because birds have better colour discrimination, chameleons need to match the background more closely to achieve a similar level of camouflage. While our results are consistent with this explanation, further experimental tests are required to verify that predators perceive the chameleon colour differences and respond to them differently. The second, not mutually exclusive explanation for better background matching in response to birds is that avian predators are more abundant. . . .*

Source: Devi Stuart-Fox, Adnan Moussalli, and Martin Whiting. "Predator-Specific Camouflage in Chameleons." Biology Letters. The Royal Society, April 29, 2008. Web. Accessed January 9, 2014.

## Consider Your Audience

Review the passage closely. How would you change the words for your teacher or your classmates? Write a blog post giving this same information to the new audience. What is the best way to get your point across to the audience?

**Common Name:** Chameleon

**Scientific Name:** *Chamaeleonidae*

**Average Size:** Four to ten inches (10 to 25 cm) long, depending on species

**Average Weight:** Up to one pound (0.5 kg), depending on species

**Color:** Green, brown, white, black, yellow, orange, red, pink, green, blue, and aquamarine

**Average Life Span:** Up to eight years in the wild, depending on species

**Diet:** Insects, larvae, small birds, reptiles, mammals, and plants

**Habitat:** Rain forests, forests, grasslands, scrublands, and deserts

**Predators:** Snakes, birds, mongooses, fossa, frogs, rats, spiders, and insects

## Did You Know?

- The eggs of the smallest chameleon species are about the size of a grain of rice.
- In rural parts of Madagascar, some people believe the myth that chameleons can blind people with their tongues.
- Chameleons are able to change colors to communicate and hide.

## Surprise Me

Learning about chameleons being able to change their colors is interesting and surprising. Think about what you learned from this book. Can you name two or three other facts about chameleons you found surprising? Write a short paragraph about each fact. Why did you find them surprising?

## Take a Stand

Chapter One talks about how chameleons can be different from each other. Think about how ground chameleons are smaller and less colorful than other chameleons. Do you think these differences mean one type is not a chameleon? Write a short essay explaining your opinion. Make sure you give reasons for your opinion. Give some evidence to support those reasons.

## You Are There

Imagine you are a scientist working in Madagascar. You are spending time researching chameleons in their natural habitats. Write 300 words about your experience. Would you want to study a chameleon's special eyes, tongues, or color-changing skills? Would you study its hunting behavior?

## Tell the Tale

Chapter Three discusses chameleon communication, hunting, and eating behaviors. Write 200 words about a day in the life of a chameleon. Remember to set the scene, develop a sequence of events, and wrap up with a conclusion.

# GLOSSARY

**arboreal**
living in or often found in trees

**camouflage**
color or shape that protects an animal from attack by making the animal difficult to see in the area around it

**captivity**
being kept in one place and not being able to leave

**extinction**
when an animal species dies out completely

**melanin**
a dark substance that is a natural part of skin, hair, and eyes

**pigment**
a natural substance that gives color to animals

**shrike**
a large bird with a hooked bill

**species**
a group of similar animals that are closely enough related to mate with one another

**territorial**
protective of a home area

**transparent**
able to be seen through

# LEARN MORE

## Books

Le Berre, François. *The Chameleon Handbook.*
  Hauppauge, NY: Barron's Educational Series,
  2009.

Morris, Neil. *African Myths.* London: Arcturus
  Publishing, 2009.

Stewart, Melissa. *How Do Chameleons Change
  Color?* Tarrytown, NY: Marshall Cavendish, 2009.

## Websites

To learn more about Amazing Reptiles, visit
**booklinks.abdopublishing.com**. These links are
routinely monitored and updated to provide the most
current information available.

Visit **www.mycorelibrary.com** for free additional tools
for teachers and students.

# INDEX

# ABOUT THE AUTHOR

Christy Devillier is an author of several nonfiction titles for young readers and has worked in book publishing for more than a decade. Christy lives in Minnesota with her family and her feisty cat, Bobo.